ALL SOULS'

All Souls'

RHEA TREGEBOV

SIGNAL EDITIONS IS AN IMPRINT OF VÉHICULE PRESS

Published with the generous assistance of The Canada Council
for the Arts and the Canada Book Fund of the Department
of Canadian Heritage.

SIGNAL EDITIONS EDITOR: CARMINE STARNINO

Cover design: David Drummond
Cover photo: Courtesy of Putnam Ladders, NYC
Photo of author: Braden Haggerty
Set in Filosofia and Minion by Simon Garamond
Printed by Marquis Book Printing Inc.

LIBRARY AND ARCHIVES CANADA CATALOGUING IN PUBLICATION

Tregebov, Rhea, 1953-
All souls' / Rhea Tregebov.

Poems.
Includes index.
ISBN 978-1-55065-338-0

I. Title.

PS8589.R342A67 2012   C811'.54   C2012-903077-5

Published by Véhicule Press, Montréal, Québec, Canada
www.vehiculepress.com

Distribution in Canada by LitDistCo
www.litdistco.ca

Distributed in the U.S. by Independent Publishers Group
www.ipgbook.com

Printed in Canada on Forest Stewardship Council certified paper.

For both beloved Sams

Contents

Family Dinners

Acknowledgements

My most sincere appreciation goes to my editor, Carmine Starnino, whose wisdom, vision and tough-mindedness have contributed so much to the quality of this book. Many darlings were dispatched to a deserved end thanks to his excellent eye and ear. To Andreas Schroeder and Sharon Brown, again, thank you for providing the refuge of your writing cottage in Roberts Creek. Thanks also to John Fanning and Kerry Eielson of La Muse Writers' Retreat in Labastide-Esparbaïrenque, Languedoc, France, for their great generosity and kindness. And thank you to the superb students in the Creative Writing Program at UBC whose passion and commitment have helped me keep the faith, in particular my thesis students: Shannon Woron, Sheryda Warrener, Natalie Thompson, Regan Taylor, Melissa Sawatsky, Kevin Spenst, Bren Simmers, Crystal Sikma, Karen Shklanka, Sandra Pettman, Elena Johnson, Ben Hart, Jamella Hagen, Amy Dennis, Amber Dawn, Emily Davidson, Brianna Brash-Nyberg, and Linda Besner. I also wish to express my gratitude to the editors of the following journals in which versions of the poems in this book have been published: *Arc, Event, Grain, Maisonneuve, The Malahat Review, The New Quarterly, Prairie Fire, Wascana Review* and the broadsheet *Poetry Strand*.

And did you get what
you wanted from this life, even so?

—RAYMOND CARVER, "Late Fragment"

D'un certain âge

The poem wakes you at seven on a Sunday.
You want to sleep. It's been a tough week.
Who knows how long you twisted
in your unsatisfactory bed after switching off

the TV. The light. At half-past midnight.
You thought all the poems had grown up
and left home. You didn't expect to find one
putting its little hands on your face.

LAND CLAIMS

All Souls' Day

Some moon – full, and fall.
So close it grazes the houses.
The clocks gone back now – six
and it's near dark. That moon
bright, though, and this city. Cars,
their lights, wash by on pavement
made for them. This sidewalk,
its dates marked in concrete
(1977, 1992), made for me.
By someone. That someone
a soul now perhaps, body
done, in earth. Winter soon.

Safe as Houses: Subprime

The system yaws and whoosh
there goes the house next door.
There goes the house on the corner,
its trim wanting a new coat.
There goes the front door,
the faces let in and let go; the mailbox
with its news, bills, dues taken in.
What was lugged up the steps,
what was tidied and swept and polished
and left in a heap. What was built.
The shelf set crooked beside the bed.
There goes morning sipping
a damn fine cup of coffee, watching
the sour-cherry tree fill the window
with bloom. What's safe now.
People are losing their homes.

September, 2008

Random

's the word for this
un-decade (the aughts,
naughts, nothings just past
century's end). Not
arbitrary, not chance, certainly
not stochastic. It works okay.
As if. Whatever. Some
friends, beer. You can't not
drift, current's way
too hard for one body:
cars blow up, buildings
blow down. Things
happen. No biggie.
It's just
how it goes.

Land Claims

Jericho Beach, Vancouver

"The beach is for everyone!"
the man snaps in hot,
inflected English. "Yes,"
the woman stiff in her Tilleys

cuts back. "The beach
is for everyone!" "Just
walk your dogs, lady. Walk
your dogs." The dogs

seem calm, sniff at the wind
as it moves across the sand, heading
east from Vancouver Island, east
over the Pacific from Asia.

Everything here is mixed up.

The sun shines blithe, just
on us here, in this city, where
we don't quite know
where we are, where

the Musqueam hold a dot of land.

It shines on binners cycling
the gravel paths, gleaning
empties in their recycled
grocery bags, saving the planet

from us, with our Nikes and
Arc'teryx, our dachshunds
and wheel-chaired relations, our
budgerigars and poodles

and gear. It shines on the walls
we've built and the ones that tumble
while above us, at 2,000 feet,
there's an eagle claiming the air.

September, 2004

Breach

In borrowed wellies and denim, I make my way through crisp stubble
to where I'm at once embattled, stomping outrigger brambles, my thick jacket
plucked by thorns as I go for the hidden shine of those globes within
globes, the darkest purple going black. I pick a way amongst and between,
and think suddenly about the deer whose path, in fact, I'm following,

who haven't boots or jackets, or, for that matter, hands –
their deft, daft tender lips, tongues, wanting the same berries I do.
What drives them to sweetness like this? I'd rather think of them
feeding poetically on roses, and forget, briefly, that roses

also have thorns, and forget, also, and then remember, what the deer did
last summer to the garden just past this field when it was its most lavish,
having found a breach, greedy, taking the saplings, the roses, hydrangea,
taking and taking till what they wanted, they destroyed. And then

remember also how, that destroyed August, years ago now, I went
by myself because nobody else wanted to, though I wanted
them to, the family I thought I had left at the cottage we'd bought
for a week. I was on the hunt then too, blueberries this time,
and went further than I ought into the thick brush by the lake,

though it was clear the bears had been there before me, all the bushes
empty, and not so clear they'd gone, or gone far. Three
green blueberries clinked into my basket, and I had nothing.
I gave up, sloped back to the dirt road the County had cleared and there,
a green wall by the ditch, thick, burdened, rich with blackberries

so everything was just in reach, nothing I'd hoped for, more
than I wanted, than I had need for, everything. And today what drives
me, who could stroll in sandals half a block down concrete to the grocer's
and buy all I want? What makes me want what is just out of reach,
drawn to difficulty, sweetness; what makes me reach for you?

Le Temps des Cerises

Massacre in my kitchen, the counter
spatter incarnadine, my hands bloodied
with the juice of cherries splayed, gutted,
for dessert at a friend's; my fingers dyed a red
that keeps in the fine creases, under the nails,
through the next day's breakfast, lunch. I tremble
to sacrifice none of this, even though the cherries, local,
organic, spoke to me, insisting on their innocence, the plump,
burgundy wholeness of them. I didn't think
to spare them, never do; not them, nor the shrimp
I clean for my son's home-coming dinner,
each shrimp life given up, given over
to our celebration. Deeper into that same night
I hear, through my open window, close,
someone else's baby cry – such grief,
and nothing will ease it, not the breast
or rest or warmth or darkness or light;
nothing will ease it forever and ever
or for the long moment till all is well
and silent. We can't help ourselves: who wouldn't trade
their own child's comfort for another's harm,
another child's harm? We can't help ourselves, knowing
it's wrong, knowing there would be a remedy
if we wanted it. Now someone has written a book
I won't be reading, about how the Earth would do without us,
rewriting not the past (airbrushing Trotsky
out of the Stalin snaps), but the future; a projection
sans project-er. It's getting hotter,
we're starting to agree we've fucked it up.
The review says the author has visited fresh
ruins, a city abandoned only decades, and it's easy
to foretell: bougainvillea purpling rooftops,

the small fingers of roots diligently rubbing out
difference. No inside; no out. To some
perhaps it's comforting to think of the Earth
scratching at its ear (*good dog!*) and us no more
than fleas in its coat: a good scrub,
a sprinkling of powder and all
is well again. None mourning our self-
massacre, not the cherries gone wild,
the gleeful shrimp gaining, all
we consumed. He imagines furthermore
humpbacks releasing their arias without contest,
butterflies sculpting air. I don't want to. Useless
though my own life has seemed to me
at times (despite cherries, despite friends), I want
this curious project to continue, our certain hunger,
our subtleties, our complicated contradictions. The arias
less necessary to me than the way a mouth is held,
the look in an eye, that engenders them. Though
my own evaluation of the human
is that, as the song goes, you can't
have one without the other.

The Gardens of the Antarctic

This is the poem that hasn't been written yet,
the one about the garden propagating itself
untended, tinting what was five million
miles square of white once green. Not
the simple ecosystem of survivors it was –
among the stone, shoals of moss,
thin lawns of hermaphrodite bryophytes,
pearlwort thickening to shelter its minute
pale yellow trumpet flowers, eking rootlets
into the chinks and pores of sandstone
and granite. Wingless, eyeless, gregarious
sprightly springtails (not bugs but dry
cousins, perhaps, of shrimp)
abounding on scree slopes. Microscopic
moss piglets rumbling a slow stroll
through lichen. Predatory mites.

Not the spare biosphere we have
and are unravelling.

Remember those elders of the other
pole, the twentieth century – the seismic
intrusion into their consciousness,
their landscape, of a bumblebee?
Next to final notice for *that* ice…
Who will be astounded by the soft rise
of what seem like groves drawing
from a soil that grew itself from penguin
guano, from the crocodilesque teeth,
the thin, articulate bones of ice-fish?

(Not yet a canopy of tree ferns, Amazonian
bromeliads lodging their small frogs, salamander,
snails. No orchids amid kapok trees, stern and sacred,
their buttressed trunks ten feet across, two
hundred high. No prickly yucca, spiders
the size of baseballs ...) Something

we can't quite picture. Something like
shrubs, their lonesome angular branches
reaching into a blur of sky, vaguely
pregnant with dwarf fruit round, red –
the evolutionary echo of a pip that
drifted south, bobbed on growlers,
the swallowed pith of an ancestor
rounder, redder. What fruit falls
among meadows of hair grass
housing the bones of whaling stations,
the pink tatting of their bloom
frayed, their blades scabbed
no longer with indigenous midges but

with alien species, things that slide, that are swift
and ragged. Rusty amid that green, and
armored. And although they may
blossom, may in their own turn
alter the air with their breath, though they
may be beautiful, this is the poem
we won't be here to read,
the one we wouldn't wish to.

Labastide-Esparbaïrenque, France

Here it is exactly: beauty and decay.
Though nothing is exact about
this town: walls as much mountain as wall,
crevices sparsely in flower. Drystone
fences marking the fields, wattle fences,
their branches laced into the grid of wire.
This place makes me think
crooked, different from the machined
thoughts of the city. Euclid was a dope.
Try to calculate the area of that irregular
field beyond the rusted railing, the garden
rough below the terrace, its order,
disorder. A pebble budges. Or
the azalea bush, spottily in bloom,
one of its bright petals shifting in a bit
of wind. The infinite perimeter of this
tuft of grass, moss on the rock below.
The distance between there and here.

Land Claims

Languedoc, France

Second run up the mountain:
walk, jog jog. Walk, jog. Walk.
It's less spooky this go round.
Here's where the road bends sharp
along the mountain's shoulder, here
its lethal drop to the right. Up ahead
the surprising log lookout askew
above the cliff. Round the next corner
and there's the gleam of metal I first
divined as a sign of habitation, and then
understood to be the ruin of a car,
windows spent, doors a-dent, wheels done.
The road rises and I slow again.
A raspy rustle to my left. A benign
dun lizard, the kind seen loafing
or skedaddling on the terrace.
It could as easily have been a snake,
even one of the infrequent *vipères*
I'm to keep an eye out for. Now
more company. A dusty butterfly
startles, lifts from a stone at my feet,
goes. This gleam of solace from other
creatures: the lie I'm not alone.

Nasturtiums

Buck twenty-nine a packet.
Plant them and wait, then
pick them. They just grow more.
Isn't that something.
You do need a buck twenty-nine.
A pot.
A spot with some sun.
But pick them, they just grow more.
Isn't that something?

Land Claims

Big Sur

Fog slips up the cliff without
even trying, changes the day.
Dogs, flies, people flit on the sand.
We want to be here. Gulls
condescend from the sky.
The surf takes the beach, takes
it again. This young woman waltzes
her baby, catches a blown sunhat
in time. A fleet of pelicans cross
in formation. We don't want pictures.

The Origin of Spices

ALLSPICE

English spice, Jamaica pepper, new spice,
clove pepper: *pimenta dioica.* Though
its names are multiple, though the scent
vows clovesnutmegginger, it's not

what it promises – all things to all people.
Home, in Jamaica, mostly untamed, un-plantationed,
it's a living, its trees growing where they will,
along fences, in thickets, wherever the seeds,

passing through bats, through birds, are released.
But the berries – the berries make things hard,
50 feet up, snipped by hand with clippers
(50 feet up!), then dried green, unripe, into pitted

petit chocolate moons, then raked and turned
in the sun, locked into sheds overnight to keep them
safe from thieves. Whole, it flavours chocolate,
cures meat, cured, once, even the dead.

CARAWAY

Indigestible *digestif*,
nipped bit in my crust of rye,
striped germ, sperm –
it is what it isn't: a seed
caught in the teeth
of the idea that flavour
is essence; a snippet
of being.

Not naught, or the
either of or, though,
kids, we thought it un-
chocolate, nothing
but a flavour, extracted,
synthetic – oozed
and looped
from a machine or,
later, baking, dripped
liquid, meted
onto a spoon. No,
it's the seed of an orchid,
bean-pod black
and crackling
to the teeth – black,
not white. Not plain,
and not good, not
the sex of the orchid –
its fruit.

Romance Sonámbulo

by Federico García Lorca

Green I want you green.
Green wind. Green branches.
Ship on the sea,
horse on the mountain.
Shadow at her waist
she dreams at her railing,
green flesh, hair green,
eyes cold silver.
Green I want you green.
Under the gypsy moon,
things are watching her
and she can't watch them.
Green I want you green.
Great stars of frost-work
come with the shadow fish
that opens the road to dawn.
The fig-tree chafes its wind
with sandpaper branches
and the hill, thieving cat,
bristles with acrid agaves.
But who will come? From where?
She stays at her railing,
green flesh, hair green,
dreaming at the bitter sea.

– Friend, I want to trade
my horse for her house,
my saddle for her mirror,
my knife for her blanket.
Friend, I come bleeding,

from the gates of Cabra.
– If I could do it, my boy,
this deal would be done.
But I am not myself any more,
and my house is not my house.
– Friend, I want to die,
decent in my bed.
Made of iron, if it could be,
with sheets of fine linen.
Don't you see the wound I have
from chest to throat?
– Your white shirtfront wears
three hundred dark roses.
Your blood oozes and reeks
around your bandage.
But I am not myself any more,
and my house is not my house.
– Let me at least climb up
to the high railings,
let me climb up! Let me
to the high railings.
Moon railings
where the water echoes.

So the two friends climb up
to the high railings.
Leaving a blood trail.
Leaving a trail of tears.
Little tin lanterns
trembled in the roof tiles.
A thousand crystal kites
wounded the dawn.

Green I want you green,
green wind, green branches.

The two friends climbed up.
The long wind left
a strange taste in the mouth
of gall, mint and basil.
– Friend! Where is she, tell me?
Where is your bitter girl?
How many times she waited for you!
How many times she would wait,
face cool, hair black,
at that green railing!

The gypsy girl rocked
on the cistern's surface.
Green skin, hair green,
eyes cold silver.
A moon icicle
holds her upon the water.
The night is intimate
as a little plaza.
Drunken *guardias civiles*
pounding on the door.
Green I want you green,
green wind, green branches.
Ship on the sea.
Horse on the mountain.

Bridge

Puzzle Box

he could (who) unravel any skein, any
of those (which) intricate difficulties
given us, or that we (what) gave ourselves,
without instruction, without (where)
solution. A patience (how) of mind, hand,
to twist and twist (when) the coloured cubes till
they settled to one (whose) plane, tone. To release
the four dull (while) enlaced bent circles, then,
diligently, turn them (whom) back into
themselves, one (if) thing. Solved. To take that closed
compartment, what was (and) sealed against itself,
each side (but) locked against the next to – presto – slide
the key component so it opened (why). He (no)
could put anything together (yes), take it apart.

Jacob

What angel were you wrestling at night,
those hours I thought we owned? I told myself
I'd bless and bless you and you'd take it

as surety, that bed we made and lay in,
take it as your due, for wasn't
I your angel to wrestle in the night?

You didn't know. What was it
you had, what was it you wanted?
Blessed and blessed again, it took

too much. Ours became the bed
you left and came to. Perhaps
there was some other angel to wrestle, nights.

I didn't know – why not? – there was a snag,
some stone within you couldn't roll aside.
To bless and be blessed and then be taken in —

was it I who wrenched your thigh? When I asked
at last at daybreak, you couldn't say your name.
If I was the angel you wrestled in the night, though
I blessed and blessed you, it didn't take.

A Guest

What touches hurts – that's
the lesson. I have this,
just below the knee, a brief
reminder of its stay, when
I also stumbled against something
harder than myself, hurrying
not to catch it, but
to let it out. For one still
moment it lighted on
the bookshelf, calm, not even
curious, as though it belonged
in a room. The bruise rainbows,
a daily show, reminder, that
I was mistaken, watching it
relinquish walls, escape back
from where it came.

Bridge

If I can't remember the name of the Pont du Gard, how will I remember
the picnic there. How will I remember the sunlight flattening every
object, pulling it into dimension. One row of arches lifting the next to
the sky and the next and then the sky with the whole day to itself,
lasting, the bricks standing and the arches letting the sky through, that
neat slice of sky. One circle of light on the river begetting an arc and
then another arc as if in play. Though it wasn't the Pont d'Avignon
(though it isn't far away), it was right there, and where was I.

Party

The get-together party fête soirée was loud boisterous noisy the canapés plentiful the hors d'oeuvres sumptuous the appetizers copious the room crowded congested aglow with candles tapers burning tealights ablaze. The city councilor was drunk the municipal representative tipsy the commissioner smashed the former radio commentator ex talk show host media personality going on about her book the hard difficult impossible tome novel best-seller albatross she hadn't been writing for twenty years. The jazz musician guitarist magnate CEO was charming loquacious garrulous a bit glib. Voluble, certainly. Funny. I ate too much. We were celebrating the birthday of someone I like. But oh the man with the beautiful wife was telling us *my wife my wife my wife* how they met the fellow with his stunning spouse was recalling their first encounter and she looked sad she looked sad she looked sad.

Standing on one foot

at the top of the stairs
holding in one hand an old
blue enamel bowl sloshing
with bright strawberries, pulling
on my sandals with the other, I stop
to know what I should know. That I shouldn't
be testing the slack-rope of this
carcass I inhabit. Plunk the foot,
the bowl, down, sit. Once I balanced
fine in a body I didn't know
was temporary. *Heel-toe, heel-toe* the trick
the physio taught my mother to keep her
walking at 85. *It's so simple,*
she says.

Bear

for William Matthews, 1942-1997

You loved
your cigarettes and steak,
didn't you? Now
I teach your poems and
they teach me but it isn't enough.
I'd rather be back at that workshop
in Paris with you, unhappy
in my marriage, having
dinner at Chez Maître Paul,
the windows open to rue
Monsieur le Prince as you
turned to blow the smoke
away from me – neither mister
nor master that warm evening,
just newfound friend. I'd rather
be there, eating *bavette à l'échalote,*
not here where you are the bear
you wrote about, gone
into anecdote.

Leaving Toronto

I'm such a sorry mess I'll miss it, I'll miss the traffic,
the exhausted diesel fuming from trucks past my bedroom window,
the bad drivers, the rude, the witless drivers, the ones who honk
as the light turns red. I'll miss my busy friends, even the ones
I hardly see, the ones who send me only Christmas letters,
the ones who don't. I'll miss dog turds rising from the black
melting ice, will miss computer spam, fax machines that smudge
only the important words. I'll miss its second-rate world-class status.
And Dufflet's. And Dooney's. All the bars I could drink in
now they've banned smoking. I'll miss my house quaking
in the streetcars' wake and the valiant dandelions and the grit
I wipe from the windowsills daily. I'll miss the spent needles and condoms
in the playground, the black squirrels chomping my crocuses.
The crocuses I'll really miss, the yellow and purple and white
white white against the grey-brown snow. I'll miss the sun as it
negotiates the smog and smear of my wide windows,
slick and smart and self-conscious across the hardwood.
Nobody will ever love this city like me.
Nobody would want to.

August, 2004

Perspective/Parallax: Love

A trick of the light
and the liner stolid in English Bay
steams steep up Trimble Street.
I'm seeing things. A trick
of the light and bull kelp
beside the ferry winks
into a sea-otter head, the dog
dead in the street twitches
back into a green garbage bag.
What am I seeing?
A trick of the light and you're
so close. So far. So close.

A Toast

Where did the bride go? She was there
in a fifth floor window, in full
confection, tugging the lip of her absurd
strapless, faceless in the particular light of this
March afternoon just as I was contemplating
marriage – specifically my long-married
friends who are still married and whom
I pray shall remain thus to the end
of days or as long as they both shall wish.
I'm in a pretty hotel room with my newly
beloved amid the bustle of float planes
in the harbour and the far gentler
roar of his sleep. The small craft
lift from the water to fly their distances
and descend. I raise a glass to them,
each take-off, each landing. Here's
to old vows, and the faith
and decency that keeps them.
And to my own parents, whom death
did part. The bride's gone from her window
to take on more poses, a bit of the Pacific
behind her, borrowed and blue. To her,
carried years past this threshold
she may believe now surely to be her life.

Reflection

The room on the other side of the glass floats
a storey above the sidewalk. Pot-lights from the ceiling
illuminate a surface perfection that ripples,
swerves with the glass. The light itself bulges.
Two empty champagne bottles preside
atop the cupboards. A parade of shape, shadowy
thin outlines of plants, bristled, align on the counter,
a dark bowl holds itself silent. And we are
not there. You're not near sleep on the sofa,
I'm not near you on the carpet, imagining
a space. The bedroom door opens to a room
behind beyond but my bed isn't there,
just the light of a room I can only with difficulty
know as across the street, real. Now we are
in this here and now we aren't are we.

Aubade

Like a dog in sleep, you
twitch, you snore. I turn you
on your side to make you stop.
Sometimes it works. This morning
you're on your back, but your breath
is soft, sun, my arm strung
across your shoulders just below
the neck. This time it's
your fingers scribbling, some tune
you're playing along the piano
of my arm, some melody.

Burden

Beast of Burden by James Wilson Morrice
[Art Gallery of Ontario]

Temple, palace – this structure
instructs us to see,
but I don't, not the beast.
Just the sweep of market,
awning, square. Parcels, heaps
of goods for sale. White
buildings, bundles. A black figure:
head, bulk of body. And that
swipe of red across the blue
and yellow sky. See burdens, bustle,
not beast. Not until I walk
to the pamphlet provided,
read the title for these forms
I haven't quite resolved
into things. And this
is what words give me,
laden: a donkey.

FAMILY DINNERS

Perspective/Parallax: Son

I picked you up. I picked you
up and put you under my arm.
I tossed you in the air.
You were that small.
Nothing had hurt you.
You didn't know hunger,
you didn't know cold.
For a little while I kept you
from harm.

Not a Mark

Not a mark on you – I checked,
that stunned first morning – not
a birthmark, not a mole
or beauty spot. Fingers,
toes, all whole and blank.
At three, shallow
dents from chicken pox
just at the right eyebrow.
At four, a scar from the hotel
night-table: you fell, screamed,
went back into sleep and only
in the morning we saw the blood
on the pillowcase. And now?
After the spill on your bike,
hell-bent down a hill trail,
the proud scrapes, greenstick
fracture of the right arm
playing touch, the burn
up the left making your own
dinner, and what else,
invisible, deeper.

The New House

You didn't like my new house. Because I packed
your childhood into two plastic bins when I moved,
and even though I followed you to your new city, I left
the old house behind, the one where we both grew up.
I packed the photo albums and your kindergarten
finger paintings, your baby clothes. I packed
the videotape of your third birthday and my fortieth.
You didn't know I was afraid to pack
everything that had been pushed to the back
of the closet – or did you? You always knew
everything, knew it often before I did, the way
tears came into your eyes but didn't fall when
your father and I sang "Ode to Joy" beside your bed,
and I thought everything was okay, I said
everything's okay, didn't I? How could I unpack
those days, remember the family you drew
for yourself before things broke –
your happy self and happy wife and happy baby.
And now here you are in the middle of your own
life, your own house – the wise life you're
constructing for yourself, for someone you love,
someone who loves you back, with work,
and friends, and food. I like my new house,
even though you're not in it often.
I want your new life, all the good things
you've put in it. Maybe I have one too.
What can we do with the old life
but make ourselves a better one?

Housework

Spring in Winnipeg, no small thing.
My parents are cleaning the windows
with vinegar, with newspapers to dry.
They stand on either side of the glass,
each other's reflection, each other's
shadow. My father on a ladder outside,
my mother in. My mother sees my father,
sees her own image faint, my father
sees only her, the window an imperfect
mirror, imperfect transparency.
Their hands move in concert
in circles from corner to centre,
steady, serious. My father
has found a spot for her, she's found
a streak for him. They're
looking after things. Soon
it will rain, soon wind will spread
the prairie dust, moths will give up
their lives against the glass, perhaps
a chickadee, perhaps a sparrow. Soon.
But now, the surface is clean.

Family Dinners: Gordie

We're eating corn on the cob. We're eating
wild rice with dried mushrooms
and my mother's pickerel fillets.
And we're remembering Granite Lake,
whose water let us see down
to those wave patterns in the bottom sand,
the shadows of the ripples on the surface
playing games with the solid ripples below.
I see my small feet, tan toes. My mother
cooking breakfast on the black woodstove.
The outdoor biffy, the canoes resting
mysteriously upside down and dry
in the boathouse. "The Smith boy," my mother asks,
"the one with hair so blond it was white,
what was his name?" "Gordie," my dad tells us.
And then we all remember the sunny afternoon
he drifted out beyond his depth, his white crew cut
sailing above the stiff orange life jacket,
that perfect boy, and his dad ran the length
of the dock, dove off, and my dad tried
running, young and strong, through the shallows
but the water held him back. "It felt like claws,"
my dad says. I see him running, see
the fierce stroke of Gordie's dad's arms,
the slow thick horror of it as both men worked
to keep the boy from something terrible.
All our mothers' warnings condensing,
their dread precipitating to the long seconds
we stood and watched, the sun and the dock
and the lake. All our mothers' warnings,
their dread, tipped over because it was fine,
they got him, he never went under. It was all

always fine. Didn't we, years too late, find
the wait on the shore, leafing through comics,
the necessary two hours after breakfast,
after lunch, as we went brown and browner,
so we wouldn't get cramps, drown, was all hooey?
"They were such a tragic family,"
my mother says, forking me some of her
pickerel. They're floured and pan-fried,
sweet with onion and she's had enough.
The sentence lies on the table in front of us.
I don't remember that part. She tells me
the dad died early, tipped over shovelling snow,
and then the mother, beyond her depth,
went under, killed herself. The pattern
of his death overlaying her life,
all she had left of it. My mother
remembers them dancing. I can taste
the clean flesh of the fish in my mouth.
It's good. That golden boy grown,
orphaned. Three of us at the table,
the rest of the family not far off,
all these years later, intact.

Family Dinners: Accident

We're eating at the fanciest restaurant anyone can imagine
in Winnipeg. We're waiting, a mite ruffled, for our mains
when they surprise us with an *amuse-bouche* – puff-pastry
with innards cheesy and tart – and we're startled
and pleased. The walls are deep blue or brick and beyond
the tall windows is the warehouse district, its sturdy old buildings
fashionable now. And the snow. It's late November.
Three weeks ago at another dinner the man I love smiled
and regaled us – me, his kids – with his birth. He was
an accident. Just twenty months between him and his older sister.
He doesn't seem to mind his haphazard entry to the world.
Now he's sitting at this capacious table with my family
and he gives us more of the story. His parents, come after the war,
failed to flourish. There were twenty-four hours, he says,
between his mother and a back-alley abortion when friends
brought to the apartment the $300 they'd gathered to take
his family through the winter. Money saved him. For that
and so many other occurrences, I have him here, close to family.
I'm just eighteen months younger than my sister, I tell him, but we
all were planned. I feel my mother rustle at my elbow.
My older sister regards me. I've heard the stories of her
lugging diaper pails. How hard it was. "Well…" my mother says.
I have a mouthful, something arcane, delicious. And feel
dislodged, suddenly the unexpected guest, no place
setting for me. How is it I didn't know, when it makes such sense?
It makes sense. I've felt always wanted and unworthy. How
is it she didn't tell me, I wail quietly across the tablecloth.
And she reminds me how her own mother broadcast
her accidental status, how little she was wanted. I want to ask
what she felt, carrying me; don't. Not yet. Remember
how welcome my own son was, from when he was a twitch
in my belly. How little her mother gave her, how much I got.
How love, unexpected, surprises.

Family Dinners: Salt and Pepper

The wooden scalloped valance
above the kitchen window in the old house
I remember, and that the window itself
framed only the white stucco wall
of the house next door. Sun through it.
Grudgingly scrubbing my little sister's
baby formula from the ridges in the chrome trim
rimming the lime-green Formica. What
I can't recollect is them together
at that table. Just my mother moving
from counter to stove to fridge, conveying
tuna casseroles and meatloaf, spaghetti
and meatballs. My father rumbling at her
from his chair to *sit down and eat.*

The valence of that orbit. What combining
power, attraction, kept them together
those years bringing us up? Bringing us
to our own lives, marriages, which we planned
on being perfect, the scratchy edges of their
irritable connection all sanded smooth.

Once we were done growing, they became our
faintly comic twosome, fitting into each others'
modest idiosyncrasies as neatly
as the paired cat and dog interlocked
in close embrace, the Dutch boy and girl,
their pouty lips never and always touching.

I know what keeps them, now. Now
my father pulls up a chair to empty
the dishwasher after it's done. Goes down
to do the laundry, taking a breather
between folds, pulling each heavy
woolen sock onto its stretcher.
My mother spoons borsht into his bowl,
tenders it to the table. He looks up,
pats at her hand, *it's so good,* betraying
what they feel still. The two
of them, together, eating dinner.

Family Dinners: Harvest

The garden's gone wild. What a summer, rain and cold.
Now, in September, we get July. I haven't been home since June,
and all I did then did nothing. I wasn't here to help.
Yanking late weeds in the heat I can think only waste,
ruin. But my mother thinks otherwise. She did
what she could do, has what she has: everywhere weeds,
yes, but also Johnny-jump-ups, Christmas roses,
calendula, bachelor's buttons amok among the beds.
Impatiens, begonia tidily abloom in their boxes. Tomatoes
my sister gave in spring as seedlings greeny still but
beginning to grow rosy. We'll take them in before frost.
Peppers just now fattening, patty-pan squash plump,
ripe, yellow. Rhubarb waving by the back fence.
Nobody noticed when the tree by the garage came down:
the gift of the neighbour's elm kept the kitchen window filled.
Come spring, my mother will sod the garden over. It's too much work.
I know. We decide to try a new recipe: chutney
made of the humblest ingredients, rhubarb and onion
stewed three hours till it comes to an unrecognizable rich
darkness. We make a meal with what we've got:
ripening tomatoes, pepper, steamed squash;
my mother's chicken spiced with the new chutney.
We make a meal, the three of us again – me, my mother,
my father with his cane, gentling himself into his chair –
the three of us still.

Family Dinners: Borrowed Time

My father can't draw the hands on the clock,
can't draw its face. In his own hand, the pencil
falters, rests. *I failed the test*, he tells us.
I look at my hands. I'd like two minutes
in our living room, Friday at 5:00, him home
and me lifted, solid, safe, beyond myself
into his hold, the feel of that hold. I'd like
ten minutes on a Sunday, January, 1959
– the length of the toboggan run down
the bank of the Red, my mother staying warm
in the car, him keeping me in the world
between his arms. An hour early June
in the back yard on Matheson Avenue,
hoeing rows for the yellow beans, the seeds
soaked, then pushed a careful fore-finger into soil.
The time it took the canoe, just big enough
to keep us, to reach the island. We were okay
with him in the stern. Then time for the fire
he made of twigs, enough to crisp five hotdogs,
one each, as we watched the light hit
the lid of the lake, glance off all it contained.

Hunger

I have your voice today on the phone,
and you somehow through it, though words
aren't working for you well. You lose my son's
name for a moment, find it. I have tone,
the music of what you are still to me.
You know I'm me. But I'm losing you in pieces.
You fell again yesterday, the faraway road
from your chair to standing. It took a long time
getting you back up. Your balance going, something
with your heart perhaps, the doctor isn't sure.
They're upping the meds. Your balance going,
your mind letting you down. You know and
don't know; tell me, joking, not joking,
you're not worth much, you're stupid.
It's not true. Though we're garbled
now. Though nothing will keep you.

Family Dinners: Spanish Rice

Unit 3-11. From his fluorescent niche
near the sorrowful eye of the nurses' station,
cinched by the tray of his Geri-chair,
a clean white terry bib the length of his chest,
my father offers a courteous spoonful.

Night

This is real, not what you wish,
not what you want. Night
outside the familiar house, doubt.
Night implacable, and also what
morning gives, which you must
accept. You're going to have to live
without someone you love, and not
because love broke. An alteration
in the landscape of what was
your life, a mountain, an ocean gone.

Family Bed

Never heard of it. And when I did I sniffed,
then snorted. I like to keep kosher: milk safe
from meat, sleep from being woken,
babies from their parents' business.
"I haven't slept in a year," my neighbour,
drawn and lovely, tells me, but each night
takes her daughter aboard the big bed. My son
flew solo in a crib in his own room because
every eyelid shift would rouse me.
I loved my sleep. My son, his father.
But today, you gone, I want not food
but that bed and in it us, father, mother,
sisters, to lay us down to sleep.

Abundance

The streets of the living are among the streets of the dead,
the houses of the living among the houses of the dead –
three centuries of dead packed close, stacked twelve deep.
On stones, scissors mark a tailor, grapes announce abundance.
The windows of the living look on, the lace of their curtains
white and clean, the leaves on their ledges potted, polished.
But the living trouble the dead: ivy, weeds
eat the stone. The acacia, maple, grow green and tall,
the berries round and red, and I can't think what their roots drink.
We tourists parade solemnly by, the pious inscribing their own messages,
slipping paper under pebbles to plead with the dead. It doesn't matter
what we want: the dead don't mind, don't care. We living get
a thick string to divide the path permitted from the path forbidden.
Two half-broken benches, a rusty tap to rinse our hands of them.

Prague, August, 2009

The epigraph by Raymond Carver is the opening lines from his poem "Late Fragment" from *All of Us: Collected Poems* (Vintage, 2000).

"Land Claims *(Jericho Beach)*": The Musqueam First Nation are descended from the Coast Salish. Their traditional territory once occupied much of what is now the city of Vancouver. Their reserve is currently adjacent to the University of British Columbia campus. In November 2007, the BC provincial government negotiated an agreement with the Band that, once finalized, will resolve three outstanding court cases regarding land rights.

"Le Temps des Cerises": The book referred to in the poem is Alan Weisman's *The World Without Us* (HarperCollins, 2007).

"The Gardens of the Antarctic": The terms used in the poem are defined as follows: *bryophyte*: non-flowering plants comprising the mosses, liverworts and hornworts which reproduce both sexually and vegetatively; some species produce both sexes on the same plant; *pearlwort*: common name for *Colobanthus quitensis,* a flowering plant native to the Antarctic which grows to about 5 cm tall; *springtail*: common name for *Cryptopygus antarcticus*, a small wingless arthropod that survives the cold by accumulating anti-freeze compounds in its body that lower the temperature at which its body freezes; *scree*: loose rock debris covering a slope; *moss piglet*: common name (along with "water bear") for *Tardigrade*, a microscopic water-dwelling, segmented animal with eight legs; *ice-fish*: there are sixteen known species of crocodile ice-fish, the common name (along with "white-blooded fish") for *Channichthyidae*, a family of fish whose blood is transparent because it contains less than 10% hemoglobin – oxygen is absorbed directly through their scaleless skin from the water; *bromeliad*: any member of the pineapple family of tropical plants, usually having stiff, leathery leaves and spikes of bright flowers;

growler: a small iceberg; *hair grass*: common name for *Deschampsia antarctica*, a fine grass native to the Antarctic.

"*Romance Sonámbulo*": Translated from the Spanish by the author from the poem by Federico García Lorca in *Obras completas* [Complete Works]. *Vols. I, II, III*, edited by Arturo del Hoyo (Aguilar, 1991).

"Bridge": The Pont du Gard is a Roman aqueduct in the South of France that was constructed to carry water to the city of Nîmes. It is thought to have been constructed in the middle of the first century A.D. It is approximately 40 km from Avignon.

"Bear": The last two lines of the poem reference Matthews' poem "The Bear at the Dump" in *Search Party: Collected Poems of William Matthews*, edited by Sebastian Matthews and Stanley Plumly (Houghton Mifflin Harcourt, 2004).

"Burden": This poem was commissioned by the Art Gallery of Ontario as part of its Ekphrasis project. The poem responds to the painting "Beast of Burden" by Canadian artist James Wilson Morrice, an oil on wood painting, 12.4 x 15.0 cm dating from around 1912–1913. This painting is part of the Thomson Collection at the Art Gallery of Ontario. James Wilson Morrice was born Montreal, Canada East (now Québec) in 1865; he died in Tunis, Tunisia, 1924. http://www.ago.net/agoid103776

"Jacob": "And Jacob was left alone; and there wrestled a man with him until the breaking of the day./ And when he saw that he prevailed not against him, he touched the hollow of his thigh; and the hollow of Jacob's thigh was out of joint, as he wrestled with him./ And he said, Let me go, for the day breaketh. And he said, I will not let thee go, except thou bless me./ And he said unto him, What is thy name? And he said, Jacob." *Genesis 32:24-27*

"Abundance": The Old Jewish Cemetery in Prague was established in the 1400s. The oldest tombstone dates from 1439. The last burial occurred in 1787. The cemetery contains approximately 12,000 tombstones and many more dead. Because space in Prague Jewish Town was limited, the dead were buried in layers. The older stones were raised as further layers were added.

Rhea Tregebov is the author of six previous books of poetry, most recently a volume of selected and new poems entitled *(alive)* (Wolsak & Wynn, 2004). She was born in Saskatoon and raised in Winnipeg. Tregebov studied literature at the universities of Manitoba, Cornell and Boston University. After living for many years in Toronto as a freelance author and editor, she moved to Vancouver to take up a position in the Creative Writing Program at the University of British Columbia in January 2005, where she is now an Associate Professor. In addition to her poetry, she has written five children's picture books. She is also the editor of numerous anthologies, including a collection of stories by women writers she co-translated from the Yiddish entitled *Arguing with the Storm*. Her first novel, *The Knife-Sharpener's Bell* (Coteau Books, 2009), won the Segal Prize in literature and was shortlisted for the 2012 Kobzar Prize.

Signal
EDITIONS

Carmine Starnino, Editor
Michael Harris, Founding Editor

THE NEW WORLD Carmine Starnino
THE LONG COLD GREEN EVENINGS OF SPRING Elisabeth Harvor
FAULT LINE Laura Lush
WHITE STONE: THE ALICE POEMS Stephanie Bolster
KEEP IT ALL Yves Boisvert (Translated by Judith Cowan)
THE GREEN ALEMBIC Louise Fabiani
THE ISLAND IN WINTER Terence Young
A TINKERS' PICNIC Peter Richardson
SARACEN ISLAND: THE POEMS OF ANDREAS KARAVIS David Solway
BEAUTIES ON MAD RIVER: SELECTED AND NEW POEMS Jan Conn
WIND AND ROOT Brent MacLaine
HISTORIES Andrew Steinmetz
ARABY Eric Ormsby
WORDS THAT WALK IN THE NIGHT Pierre Morency
    (Translated by Lissa Cowan and René Brisebois)
A PICNIC ON ICE: SELECTED POEMS Matthew Sweeney
HELIX: NEW AND SELECTED POEMS John Steffler
HERESIES: THE COMPLETE POEMS OF ANNE WILKINSON, 1924-1961
    Edited by Dean Irvine
CALLING HOME Richard Sanger
FIELDER'S CHOICE Elise Partridge
MERRYBEGOT Mary Dalton
MOUNTAIN TEA Peter Van Toorn
AN ABC OF BELLY WORK Peter Richardson
RUNNING IN PROSPECT CEMETERY Susan Glickman
MIRABEL Pierre Nepveu (Translated by Judith Cowan)
POSTSCRIPT Geoffrey Cook
STANDING WAVE Robert Allen
THERE, THERE Patrick Warner
HOW WE ALL SWIFTLY: THE FIRST SIX BOOKS Don Coles
THE NEW CANON: AN ANTHOLOGY OF CANADIAN POETRY
    Edited by Carmine Starnino
OUT TO DRY IN CAPE BRETON Anita Lahey
RED LEDGER Mary Dalton
REACHING FOR CLEAR David Solway
OX Christopher Patton
THE MECHANICAL BIRD Asa Boxer
SYMPATHY FOR THE COURIERS Peter Richardson
MORNING GOTHIC: NEW AND SELECTED POEMS George Ellenbogen
36 CORNELIAN AVENUE Christopher Wiseman
THE EMPIRE'S MISSING LINKS Walid Bitar
PENNY DREADFUL Shannon Stewart
THE STREAM EXPOSED WITH ALL ITS STONES D.G. Jones
PURE PRODUCT Jason Guriel
ANIMALS OF MY OWN KIND Harry Thurston
BOXING THE COMPASS Richard Greene
CIRCUS Michael Harris
THE CROW'S VOW Susan Briscoe
WHERE WE MIGHT HAVE BEEN Don Coles
MERIDIAN LINE Paul Bélanger (Translated by Judith Cowan)
SPINNING SIDE KICK Anita Lahey
GIFT HORSE Mark Callanan
THE SMOOTH YARROW Susan Glickman
SUMPTUARY LAWS Nyla Matuk
ALL SOULS' Rhea Tregebov